THE
BOOK ON SOCIAL SECURITY DISABILITY

A Practical Guide to
Obtaining your Disability Benefits

Jason Harmon, Esq.
Tiffany Tate Logan, Esq.
Clara Van Horn, Esq.

Ascend Legal Publishing
5500 Prytania St., #421
New Orleans, LA 70115
504.533.8784

ISBN: 978-0-578-20234-1 (sc)
ISBN: 978-0-578-20569-4 (ebook)

Rev. date: 11/16/2018

DEDICATION

This book is dedicated to those who are suffering. Although you may struggle in silence, you are not alone. Keep fighting!

It is dedicated to my Bird, who has been next to me serving and fighting the good fight since our mission was only an idea. You were there from the beginning, and will be there at the end.

It is dedicated to Sue & Eddie, who could not wait to meet me over three decades ago. You have offered a lifetime of support and encouragement. Where has the time gone?

Last, but certainly not least, it is dedicated to the amazing people with whom I work, particularly the co-authors of this book, Tiffany and Clara. You two make Ascend what it is. You work tirelessly to serve our people. I could not ask for more intelligent, accomplished, and compassionate attorneys to stand shoulder to shoulder with on the front line. Shields ready. Swords drawn. Non nobis solum nati summus! ("Not for ourselves alone are we born.")[1]

---

[1] Marcus Tullius Cicero

CONTENTS

Dedication.. v
Preface ix
Who this Book is For... xv
Why this Book is Necessary... xvii
Disclaimer (Warning: Lawyer-Speak Ahead)...................... xix
A Note on Legal Citations.. xxi
Introduction... xxiii

Chapter 1   Social Security Disability Insurance and
Supplemental Security Income 1

Chapter 2   How the Social Security Administration Decides
Disability—The 5-Step Sequential Evaluation Process 4

Chapter 3   Substance Abuse & Failure to Follow Prescribed
Treatment—Two Things that Can Get You Denied
Regardless of the Severity of Your Medical Condition..... 19

Chapter 4   How the Process Works 22

Chapter 5   Filing the Initial Application 27

Chapter 6   The Hearing & the Administrative Law Judge 31

Chapter 7   The Appeals Council... 34

Chapter 8   Proving Your Case.. 35

Chapter 9   Credibility—A Term of Art.. 37

Chapter 10   How to Speed Things Up... 39

Chapter 11   How a Lawyer Can Help.. 42

Chapter 12   Clients Rights and Responsibilities
at Ascend Disability... 44

About the Author.. 49

PREFACE
BY JASON HARMON

"The purpose of life is not to be happy. It is to be useful, to be honorable, to be compassionate, to have it make some difference that you have lived and lived well."
—Ralph Waldo Emerson

I represented one of my first Social Security Disability claimants when I was 25-years old. It was a nerve-racking, heart-breaking, awe-inspiring, and life-changing experience. More on that in a moment. First, I must provide some context. When I graduated college, I was searching for meaning. I had absolutely no idea what I wanted to do, and little idea of what I was good at. As a young man, I was beginning to understand what it meant to struggle to provide for myself. I double majored in English and Psychology, and while I have found that education to be invaluable in the course of my career, those degrees did not present a great deal of immediate, put-bread-on-the-table type of opportunity. So, as most young men and women do when they are searching for a vocation, I just took what was available. I needed a J-O-B that would pay the bills. A vocation would have to wait.

During college I worked as a runner at a local law firm and enjoyed the people with whom I worked—from the wonderful elderly lady in the mailroom, Ruth,[2] to the VP of Operations. The founder had an amazing, entrepreneurial mind, and was constantly growing different facets of

---

[2] Ruth, if you ever read this, I want you to know that I still appreciate the opportunity that I had to work with you. You are one of the hardest-working and most loyal co-workers whom I have ever had the privilege of working beside. I will never forget the stories you told me of your youth during World War II, of waiting at the train station with flowers for the soldiers arriving by rail car. I continue to admire your

the firm and his business. While this was chaotic, it offered a lot of opportunity and excitement for those who wanted it. I wrote blog articles for the website, filed paperwork, worked in the intake department helping prospective clients, created procedural manuals, scanned incoming mail, put desks together, and even painted offices. It was all hands on deck trying to get the job done. After graduation, I went to my bosses and asked for more responsibility. They were gracious enough to give me a chance, but first I had to pay my dues.

My first duty related to Social Security Disability was organizing and scanning hundreds of pages of medical records under the supervision of a very experienced paralegal, who was a nurse by trade, and who had assisted thousands of individuals with their disability claims. I sat in the office two feet across the hall from her, surrounded by a mountain of incoming paper. I went through every page, organized it, scanned it, and then filed it, until my eyes felt like they were going to bleed. While the job was incredibly monotonous, unbeknownst to me at the time, it was the beginning of a true vocation. I was absorbing a continuous flow of data, and was beginning to understand the most important aspect of a disability case—the medical evidence. I was also blessed to work next to someone who had over a decade of experience in this area of law. I learned to never underestimate the power of observation and listening. My work days were spent scanning, filing, and listening, with an emphasis on the latter.

As my knowledge grew, my thirst for information grew. I read everything about disability that I could get my hands on, including legal treatises, industry publications, consumer books, and redacted legal briefs that had been submitted in prior cases. My library began to grow, burgeoning with all of the most important publications used by practitioners in the industry. Ultimately, I started to edit all of the briefs that were being submitted for upcoming hearings. I read hundreds of legal arguments and reviewed an equivalent number of medical evidence outlines.

This firehose of information, both technical and practical, allowed me to begin writing my own briefs. As the practice grew, so did I, and

work ethic and your willingness to sacrifice yourself for others. I hope that you are well. Your memory has remained with me all these years.

I was promoted to the position of Case Manager, which allowed me to begin working with actual human beings, who were suffering from very real physical and mental medical conditions. They were no longer just names in medical records. They became real to me, and that is when my life changed. When you are surrounded by human suffering on a daily basis, you experience it vicariously, even though you are not fighting the same battle. It becomes part of your world and resides in the subconscious. I started to look at life through a different lens. This new world was one of both despair and hope, and it gave me that thing that I had been lacking during my college years—purpose.

Back to my first hearing. I had been working with our client, who we will call Molly for over a year.[3] She suffered from a severe mental health condition that caused auditory and visual hallucinations, extreme paranoia, and delusions. Her mind had been ravaged by the disease process to the point that she was locking herself in her room at night to avoid hurting her husband of 20 years. During psychotic episodes she heard terrifying voices instructing her to hurt others and herself. She believed that people were out to get her. She would see aberrations and malevolent shadows chasing and following her. Afraid of what she might do to herself or her husband, she would sleep in a separate bedroom in which she isolated herself for up to a week without eating or bathing.

By the time we got to her hearing I had fully reviewed all of her medical evidence, and understood what her condition looked like from a technical standpoint. It was a sterile, mechanical understanding, the type of understanding needed to discuss the legal merits of the case with an experienced Administrative Law Judge. I remember being so nervous about failing Molly, that I stayed up all night drinking coffee and rehearsing my line of questioning. When I arrived at the hearing office, however, and met she and her husband, the anxiety resolved. She was a small thing, no more than five feet tall, with hazy brown eyes, and straight raven-black hair. As I extended my hand and introduced myself, she politely, and somewhat nervously responded without making eye contact. I could see that she had been crying, as her mascara blurred unevenly at the outer edges. She clung to her husband's arm as if she were

---

[3] The client's name and certain facts, diagnoses, and symptoms have been changed to protect the client's identity.

hanging on for dear life. He shook my hand, and in a West Texas drawl, said: "It is so great to meet you Mr. Harmon. We've been waiting for this day for a long time."

We entered the court room and the hearing proceeding began. I questioned my client about all of her symptoms, medical treatment, past work, difficulties holding jobs, problems with maintaining personal hygiene, hallucinations, thoughts of suicide, side effects of medication, and everything else that was supported by the evidence in the file. Her testimony was okay, but I felt that she was holding back to protect herself from revealing too much to the strangers in the room. She did not want people to truly know the depth of her condition. I sensed her reluctance, so I had to get testimony from her husband.

Holding back tears, he told her to show us her stomach. Reluctantly, the judge allowed it. She raised her shirt, revealing a patchwork of deep gashes and scars longitudinally across her entire stomach. They resembled the claw marks of a wild animal that had tried to tear her open. The room was silent. Her husband explained that, when she was very depressed, she would use knives, razor blades, and her own fingernails to cut herself. Over time, these gashes had developed so much scar tissue that her abdomen appeared to be one big scar. Then he told her to show us her arms. She complied, slowly pulling back her long sleeves that she used to hide the evidence. Her arms had similar scars and gashes, with multiple large, deep scars at her wrists. After my client refused to explain the injuries, her husband told the judge that those were the scars of past suicide attempts. I knew from the evidence that she had a history of self-harm and suicide attempts, but it is nearly impossible to understand what that looks like in real life. Those physical scars represented the deep, pathological, emotional turmoil that she lived with on a daily basis. They also represented her husband's battles.

I do not tell this story for shock value. I tell it to illustrate the power that hope and love have to sustain us, even in the midst of such terrible anguish. Before the judge closed the hearing, Molly said that the only thing keeping her alive was her husband. He remained at the table with her, and reached across to hold her hand tightly. They both cried, but only looked at each other as they did so, and Molly smiled for the first time at the hearing. Whatever happened, he still loved her, as he had for the prior two decades before her disease had consumed her. She was still his Molly—the same Molly he picked up in his old beat-up pickup for their first date 20 years prior.

This experience was a turning point in my life. I finally understood what it meant to be an advocate for someone. I understood what sacrifice meant. The sacrifice that this man made to care for his disabled wife, the love of his life, had a profound impact on me.

I went on to get my law degree, but always stayed close to this field of practice, and eventually opened my own law firm. While I have now represented thousands of clients and attended hundreds of hearings, this memory stays with me. It represents a coming-of-age in my life, but more importantly, a change in my world view that has since been further developed by the stories of thousands of other disabled individuals. Nearly 15 years later, my mind is filled with an endless track of these stories. They are stories of despair, hope, tragedy, resilience, love, and loss. This track represents humanity to me, and it will forever be with me. Through this work, I have been given the great privilege of walking through life with so many wonderful people, who are going through a hard time, and I am eternally grateful for it.

WHO THIS BOOK IS FOR

This book is primarily written for the man or woman who is no longer able to work due to serious injury or illness. It is for the worker who has tried and given it his or her all, but can no longer continue working. This book is for the disabled worker.

The term "disabled" is a loaded word, and it can mean many different things depending on the context. It has societal connotations, legal connotations, and even moral connotations, but for purposes of this book, "disabled" means that one can no longer perform the essential functions of his or her past work, and that a serious medical condition significantly limits one's ability to perform other work in the economy.

This book is for the 55-year old welder who has a herniated lumbar disc, the 50-year-old secretary with severe carpal tunnel syndrome, the 35-year old delivery driver with severe congestive heart failure, and the 45-year old nurse assistant with debilitating Bipolar Disorder. It is for family and friends who want to assist their loved ones in navigating the life-altering challenges associated with severe physical or mental illness.

WHY THIS BOOK IS NECESSARY

We wrote this book as a general guide to help individuals navigate the daunting process of applying for and receiving disability benefits. The path is neither straight, nor quick for most people, and it takes a significant amount of perseverance to make it to the end. One must deal with the world's largest judicial bureaucracy—the Social Security Administration—while managing doctor's appointments, dealing with severe physical and mental symptoms, and meeting the basic necessities of life. It is not easy, but it can be done. This book is designed to help one develop a strong case that is more likely to get approved.

It may also be useful to those who are not currently disabled, but who are beginning to have difficulty maintaining employment. In addition to sudden injuries that immediately put people out of work, many individuals suffer from long-standing illnesses or injuries that become worse with age and repetitive physical activity. These disabilities happen slowly and almost imperceptibly, but the symptoms become more apparent over time. A back problem that has caused one to be out of work or to undergo surgery in the past becomes unbearable, and the worker misses an increasing number of workdays. A heart condition has always been controlled with medication, but the individual begins to have more shortness of breath, swelling, and chest pain that no longer responds to increasing dosages of medication. One's diabetes has been relatively stable, but he begins to experience increasing levels of neuropathy in the legs, feet, arms, and hands. Except in cases where there has been a workplace accident or a sudden injury, the moment that one becomes "disabled" is rarely a fine line.

Finally, this book is for the proactive person who is prepared to fight. If you are still reading, you are likely that person. Even with a lawyer, the most successful outcomes go to those who participate in their recovery and planning. This book is for the fighters. We are engaging in disaster preparedness planning, where worst case scenarios must be contemplated. It will take mental fortitude, excellent preparation, often times a really good attorney, and certainly a little bit of luck.

DISCLAIMER (WARNING: LAWYER-SPEAK AHEAD)

We are lawyers, and as such, we have to follow a lot of rules that the general public and other types of businesses are not required to follow. While we do not want to insult the reader's intelligence, we must comply with specific rules of ethics for our state bar and other state bars. So, forgive us in advance, but we must tell you that this book does not constitute legal advice, and should not be relied upon as such. Without knowing the particulars of your situation and retaining you as a client, it is impossible for us to advise you in particular legal matters. This book also constitutes a written communication from a lawyer, and as such, we also have to tell you that this does not create an attorney-client relationship. Mind-blowing stuff, I know! This is why people do not like to communicate with lawyers!

Now that you know we are not your attorneys, that this book is not legal advice, and that you should contact an attorney if you have legal questions regarding the particulars of your situation, we can tell you to read, reread, highlight, and outline this book. The more you know, the more prepared you will be to navigate the rough seas ahead.

A NOTE ON LEGAL CITATIONS

We have written this book as a practical manual for the average consumer. Pertinent law, regulations, and rulings are referenced should the reader require more detail, but they do not follow the Bluebook or ALWD Citation Manual. I have also cited SSDI regulations only, and not SSI regulations. The reader will notice footnotes citing regulations beginning with 20 CFR § 404. These citations reference the SSDI program only. SSI regulations are found in 20 CFR § 416. SSDI regulations begin at 20 CFR § 404.15012. SSI regulations start at 20 CFR § 416.901. To find the correlating SSI regulation, you take 416.9 and add the last two digits of the cited SSDI regulation. For example, in Chapter 2 of this book, I cite the definition of disability found in 20 CFR § 404.1505. To find the ancillary SSI regulation, you simply take "416.9" and add "05" to the end to get 416.905.

INTRODUCTION

"One must lie low, no matter how much it went against the grain, and try to understand that this great organization remained, so to speak, in a state of delicate balance, and that if someone took it upon himself to alter the dispositions of things around him, he ran the risk of losing his footing and falling to destruction, while the organization would simply right itself by some compensating reaction in another part of its machinery — since everything interlocked — and remain unchanged, unless, indeed, which was very probable, it became still more rigid, more vigilant, severer, and more ruthless."

— Franz Kafka, The Trial

Welcome to the Social Security Administration, the world's largest administrative judicial system. Like all good bureaucracies, it is designed with one over-arching principal in mind—efficiency. The beauty of individual humanity is not permitted inside its walls, although many Judges and agency representatives do their best to tuck it into their briefcases and secret into their chambers.

There is something about bureaucracy that is necessary, namely, that it creates order. President Roosevelt once said that "order without justice and justice without order are equally destructive." The SSA has taken this to heart, putting an emphasis on "order," even though justice is a worthy and stated program goal. It is hard to blame them when one looks at the staggering amount of new claims that are filed every year, the growing backlog of over 1 million appeals awaiting hearing,[4] and the lack of budgetary increases necessary to provide the additional infrastructure and staff necessary to handle the workload. From a 30,000 foot view, the

---

[4] As of 2018

disability determination process is an assembly line in which different people and agencies handle different components of the work involved. Like all assembly lines, it is designed to be as efficient as possible.

Due largely to the aging baby boomer generation and the increasing number of women who began entering the workforce in the 1960's, this bureaucracy is under a tremendous amount of stress. The baby boomer generation is the largest population increase in our nation's history, and while that is good for gross domestic product and remaining competitive in the global economy, it causes a big problem for mid-20th century national programs designed to take care of our sick and elderly. Now that all of our baby boomers are hitting the age where people begin having more medical problems, their huge population is creating a tremendous draw on the trust fund.

There is also a much larger population of women who qualify for these benefits now, because the later part of the Civil Rights Movement brought with it increased job opportunity for women, and a cultural shift began in which more and more women entered the workforce. There are other factors that periodically impact the trust fund's solvency, such as large economic downturns, like the one we experienced in 2008, in which vast numbers of jobs are eliminated from the economy, pushing people to look for other options to support their families.

Because of the perfect storm in which we now find ourselves, it has become much harder to qualify for benefits, as evidenced by the drastically declining approval rating over the last decade. As such, it is important to understand the decision-making process, the best way to prepare a case, and the timeframe involved. You cannot go into this without a Plan B. This is not a quick or certain solution to your financial and vocational difficulties. If you can work, give it your all, because this program may not sustain you in the future. It is a last resort.

THE

BOOK ON

SOCIAL

SECURITY

DISABILITY

CHAPTER 1

Social Security Disability Insurance and Supplemental Security Income

"No one is useless in this world who lightens the burdens of another."

—Charles Dickens

There are a number of programs available to the disabled worker, but this book focuses on SSDI and SSI. The Old Age, Survivors, and Disability Insurance program provides monetary and health benefits to those who become injured and who also paid Social Security taxes while they were employed. Social Security Disability Insurance (SSDI) benefits fall under this program. Those who did not pay into the Social Security fund through taxes may be eligible for Supplemental Security Income (SSI), which is a public assistance program. SSDI and SSI use the same medical and legal decision-making process, but they have different non-medical technical requirements.

Social Security Disability Insurance

In order to be eligible for SSDI, most people must have acquired 20 quarters of coverage in the 40-quarter period leading up to the quarter in which the disability began. This is commonly referred to as the 20/40 rule. This requirement is typically satisfied if you have worked and paid Social Security taxes for at least 5 out of the last 10 years. This is a basic technical threshold that you must pass before your medical condition will be evaluated by the Social Security Administration (SSA).

There are other differences as well. The amount of your monthly benefits is based on the amount of FICA contributions that you have made. Furthermore, household income and resources do not affect your benefit amount. Unlike SSI, you may also receive retroactive benefits payments up to a year prior to your application date.

IMPORTANT DIFFERENCES BETWEEN SSDI AND SSI

Both programs have the same definition of disability: You must have a physical or mental medical condition that prevents you from working and that has lasted or is expected to last for 12 months or longer, or results in death.

However, there are some important differences in the two programs. Some of the main differences are listed below.

	SSDI	SSI
Work Credits vs. Resources	You must have worked and paid a sufficient amount into the trust fund to earn 20 work credits out of the last 40 quarters. Most people satisfy this requirement if they have worked and paid into the system at least 5 out of the last 10 years. It is also available for certain qualifying relatives. Household income and resources do not affect eligibility for SSDI.	SSI is a needs-based program and you do not need work credits. You need to be below certain income and resource levels. The resource limit for individuals is $2,000, and for married couples is $3,000. It is not available for relatives.
Monthly Benefit Amount	Benefit amount is based on the amount of FICA contributions.	Benefit amount is the Federal Benefit Rate. Some states also add an additional supplement.
Effect of Household Income and Resources	Do not affect the amount of monthly benefits that one can receive.	Can affect eligibility and the monthly benefit amount.
Retroactive Benefits	Benefits can be paid retroactively. They typically begin five months after the onset of disability and can be paid up to 12 months prior to the application date.	Benefits begin the 1st of the month after the month in which the application is filed.
Health Insurance	Beneficiaries automatically qualify for Medicare after 24 months of eligibility.	Beneficiaries qualify for Medicaid immediately.
Monthly Payment Schedule	The date upon which individuals are paid each month varies depending on birth date, except for instances in which people are receiving both SSDI and SSI benefits at the same time.	Benefits are paid on the first of the month each month.

ASCEND
DISABILITY LAWYERS LLC

Supplemental Security Income (SSI)

SSI on the other hand is a needs-based program. One does not need to have acquired work credits for this program. Rather, you must be below certain income and resource limits. Income is anything that one receives in cash or "in kind" that can be used to provide food or shelter. A resource is cash, real property, or anything that can be converted to cash and used for support and maintenance. The SSA distinguishes between earned and unearned income. Earned income includes wages, self-employment, and several other sources, and unearned income is essentially everything else.

In order to pass the technical requirements to receive SSI benefits, a single individual cannot have more than $2,000 in resources, and a married couple cannot have more than $3,000 in resources. However, there are some very important resources that are excluded in this calculation, including an individual's home and one car among other things.

Not only can income and resources affect one's ability to qualify for SSI benefits, but it can also decrease the monthly benefit amount. In most cases, there will be a dollar for dollar deduction for income. If it is "in-kind" income—that is, food or shelter—the SSA can reduce one's benefit amount by up to one third.

Social Security also counts the income and resources of a disabled worker's spouse. Through a complicated process called deeming, about which we will not go into great detail, the SSA may count the income and resources of a spouse as income or resources that can either reduce the benefit amount or make one ineligible for benefits all together.

In summary, if you have paid into the Social Security fund long enough and recently enough, you will have enough work credits to apply for SSDI benefits. If you have either not worked long enough or recently enough, or you worked but did not pay into the system, you may still be eligible for SSI benefits if your household income and resources are below the limit. Sometimes it is even advisable to apply for both programs. An experienced lawyer may be able to assist you in determining which program you should apply for.

CHAPTER 2

How the Social Security Administration Decides Disability—The 5-Step Sequential Evaluation Process

"Order and simplification are the first steps towards mastery of a subject."

—Mann

Understand the 5-Step Sequential Evaluation Process, and you understand how claims are decided. While volumes have been written on the nuances of this area of law, the average person needs only to understand the five steps. They are applied in order during every phase of the decision-making process, and bring an element of simplicity to very complex subject matter.

Social Security defines disability as the "inability to engage in any substantial gainful activity by reason of any medically determinable physical or mental impairment which can be expected to result in death or which has lasted or can be expected to last for a continuous period of not less than 12 months."[5] There you have it. You must have a physical or mental medical condition that prevents you from working and that has lasted or is expected to last for 12 months or longer, or results in death.

In order to evaluate whether you meet this definition of disability, and are entitled to benefits, the SSA has established a five-step sequential evaluation process that is designed to promote uniformity in the decision-making process.[6] At each step, except for step 3, your claim may be denied.

---

[5] 20 CFR § 404.1505
[6] 20 CFR § 404.1520

5 STEP SEQUENTIAL EVALUATION PROCESS

1 ### Is the claimant performing substantial gainful activity?
YES: Denied   NO: Continue to next step ▼

2 ### Is the claimant's medical condition severe within the meaning of the regulations?
YES: Continue to next step ▼   NO: Denied

3 ### Does the claimant's medical condition meet or equal a Listing
YES: Approved for Benefits   NO: Continue to next step ▼

RFC Assessment
SSA then assesses the individual's Residual Functional Capacity: what she can still do despite her limitations.
No determination made at this step.

4 ### Considering the individual's RFC, can she perform her past relevant work (PRW)
YES: Denied   NO: Continue to next step ▼

5 ### Considering the individual's RFC, age, education, and work experience, are there other jobs in the economy that she can do?
YES: Denied   NO: Approved for Benefits

ASCEND
DISABILITY LAWYERS LLC

If you meet the requirements of Step 3, your claim is approved and you will be deemed disabled under the regulations. If you do not meet the requirements of Step 3, the evaluation process continues through the remainder of the steps.

Step 1: Substantial Gainful Activity (SGA)

At Step 1 they look at your work activity to determine whether or not you are performing "substantial gainful activity."[7] While there are several ways to make this determination, the most widely used is to simply look at your income from work activity. The statutory amount for 2018 is $1,180.00. For blind individuals, the amount is $1,970.00. If you earn this amount or more, you are engaging in substantial gainful activity, and your claim will be denied. If you earn less, or you are not working, the process continues to the next step.

Step 2: Severity

At Step 2 they must decide whether your physical or mental medical condition is "severe." This definition has two parts, a functional part and a temporal part. A severe physical impairment is one that significantly limits your ability to perform basic work activities, such as standing, walking, sitting, lifting, pushing, pulling, reaching, carrying, and handling, among other things.[8] Mental aptitudes necessary to perform gainful work include understanding, carrying out, and remembering simple instructions, the use of judgment, responding appropriately to supervision, co-workers and usual work situations, and dealing with routine changes in a work setting. In some instances you may have multiple conditions that are not severe when considered alone, but the combined effects of the different impairments may be severe enough to prevent you from working.[9]

For purposes of passing this step, the bar is fairly low, and you will only be denied if you have a very minor impairment. However, some people run into trouble with the second part of this definition, which

---

[7] 20 CFR § 404.1510
[8] 20 CFR § 404.1522
[9] 20 CRF § 404.1523

includes the durational requirement. A disability must have lasted or be expected to last for at least a year, or result in death. For example, if you suffer a back injury that causes you to stop working, and you have to undergo surgery and an extensive recovery period, you may be unable to work during that time. Your condition may prevent you from engaging in basic work activities, like standing, walking, or sitting. However, if you regain functioning and improve enough to be able to work prior to 12 months having passed since your injury, your condition will be considered non-severe, and you will be denied. In some cases, if your condition lasts a year or more, but you ultimately regain enough functional ability to go back to work, you may be eligible for a "closed period" of benefits for the period of time that your condition prevented you from working. In those cases you will be awarded benefits for that period only, and will not receive on-going monthly benefits.

Step 3: Meeting or Equaling a Listing

If the SSA determines that your condition is severe, they will then consider whether you meet or equal a "Listing" identified in the Listing of Impairments. The SSA has compiled a non-exhaustive list of impairments it considers to be disabling. The Listings consist of medical conditions and findings that are suggestive of a gravely disabling condition, and offer an opportunity to be found disabled without having to make determinations at Steps 4 and 5 of the evaluation process. The Listings are broken down into the 14 different body systems listed below:

- 1.00 Musculoskeletal
- 2.00 Special Senses and Speech
- 3.00 Respiratory Disorders
- 4.00 Cardiovascular System
- 5.00 Digestive System
- 6.00 Genitourinary Disorders
- 7.00 Hematological Disorders
- 8.00 Skin Disorders
- 9.00 Endocrine Disorders
- 10.00 Congenital Disorders that Affect Multiple Body Systems

- 11.00 Neurological Disorders
- 12.00 Mental Disorders
- 13.00 Cancer (Malignant Neoplastic Diseases)
- 14.00 Immune System Disorders

These systems are then broken down into specific disease processes, under which very particular criteria must be met. For example, Listing 1.00 covers the Musculoskeletal System. Within that Listing are subcategories for specific impairments like Disorders of the Spine (1.04). That category is broken down into even more granular criteria that must be met.

In circumstances where an individual has an impairment not specifically identified in the Listings, you may be found disabled at this step by "equaling" the listing if you exhibit symptoms or limitations that are of equal severity as the criteria contained in the Listing.[10]

Most people do not have medical conditions that are as severe as those contemplated in the Listings. Nevertheless, they can still be found disabled by showing that they cannot perform their past work or other work. As such, a finding that you do not meet a Listing does not result in a denial. The process simply proceeds to the next steps.

---

[10] 20 CFR § 404.1526

LISTING OF IMPAIRMENTS

1.00 Musculoskeletal System
1.02 Major Dysfunction of a Joint(s) (Due to Any Cause)
1.03 Reconstructive Surgery or Surgical Arthrodesis of a Major Weight-Bearing Joint
1.04 Disorders of the Spine
1.05 Amputation (Due to Any Cause)
1.06 Fracture of the Femur, Tibia, Pelvis, or One or More of the Tarsal Bones
1.07 Fracture of an Upper Extremity
1.08 Soft Tissue Injuries

2.00 Special Senses and Speech
2.02 Loss of Central Visual Activity
2.03 Contraction of the Visual Fields in the Better Eye
2.04 Loss of Visual Efficiency
2.07 Disturbance of Labyrinthine-Vestibular Function
2.09 Loss of Speech
2.10 Hearing Loss Not Treated with Cochlear Implantation
2.11 Hearing Loss Treated with Cochlear Implantation

3.00 Respiratory Disorders
3.02 Chronic Respiratory Disorders
3.03 Asthma
3.04 Cystic Fibrosis
3.07 Bronchiectasis
3.09 Chronic Pulmonary Hypertension Due to Any Cause
3.11 Lung Transplant
3.14 Respiratory Failure

4.00 Cardiovascular System
4.02 Chronic Heart Failure
4.04 Ischemic Heart Disease
4.05 Recurrent Arrhythmias
4.06 Symptomatic Congenital Heart Disease
4.09 Heart Transplant
4.10 Aneurysm of Aorta or Major Branches
4.11 Chronic Venous Insufficiency
4.12 Peripheral Arterial Diseases

5.00 Digestive System
5.02 Gastrointestinal Hemorrhaging from Any Cause, Requiring Blood Transfusion
5.05 Chronic Liver Disease
5.06 Inflammatory Bowel Disease (IBD)
5.07 Short Bowel Syndrome (SBS)
5.08 Weight Loss Due to Any Digestive Disorder
5.09 Liver Transplant

6.00 Genitourinary Disorders
6.03 Chronic Kidney Disease, with Chronic Hemodialysis or Peritoneal Dialysis
6.04 Chronic Kidney Disease, with Kidney Transplant
6.05 Chronic Kidney Disease, with Impairment of Kidney Function
6.06 Nephrotic Syndrome
6.09 Complications of Chronic Kidney Disorder

ASCEND
DISABILITY LAWYERS LLC

LISTING OF IMPAIRMENTS (continued)

7.00 Hematological Disorders
7.05 Hemolytic Anemias, Including Sickle Cell Disease, Thalassemia, & Their Variants
7.08 Disorders of Thrombosis & Hemostasis
7.10 Disorders of Bone Marrow Failure
7.17 Hematological Disorders Treated by Bone Marrow or Stem Cell Transplantation
7.18 Repeated Complications of Hematological Disorders

8.00 Skin Disorders
8.02 Ichthyosis
8.03 Bullous Disease
8.04 Chronic Infections of the Skin or Mucous Membranes
8.05 Dermatitis
8.06 Hidradenitis Suppurativa
8.07 Genetic Photosensitivity Disorders
8.08 Burns

9.00 Endocrine Disorders
9.01 Pituitary Gland Disorders
9.02 Thyroid Gland Disorders
9.03 Parathyroid Gland Disorders
9.04 Adrenal Gland Disorders
9.05 Diabetes Mellitus and Other Pancreatic Gland Disorders
9.05(a) Hyperglycemia
9.05(a)(i) Diabetic Ketoacidosis
9.05(a)(ii) Chronic Hyperglycemia
9.05(b) Hypoglycemia

10.00 Congenital Disorders That Affect Multiple Body Systems
10.01 Mosaic Down Syndrome and Other Congenital Disorders That Affect Multiple Body Systems
10.06 Non-Mosaic Down Syndrome
10.06(a) Chromosome 21 Trisomy
10.06(b) Chromosome 21 Translocation

11.00 Neurological Disorders
11.02 Epilepsy
11.04 Vascular Insult to the Brain
11.05 Benign Brain Tumors
11.06 Parkinsonian Syndrome
11.07 Cerebral Palsy
11.08 Spinal Cord Disorders
11.09 Multiple Sclerosis
11.10 Amyotrophic Lateral Sclerosis (ALS)
11.11 Post-Polio Syndrome
11.12 Myasthenia Gravis
11.13 Muscular Dystrophy
11.14 Peripheral Neuropathy
11.17 Neurodegenerative Disorders of the Central Nervous System, Such as Huntington's Disease, Friedreich's Ataxia, and Spinocerebellar Degeneration
11.18 Traumatic Brain Injury
11.20 Coma or Persistent Vegetative State
11.22 Motor Neuron Disorders Other Than ALS

ASCEND
DISABILITY LAWYERS LLC

LISTING OF IMPAIRMENTS (continued)

12.00   Mental Disorders
12.02   Neurocognitive Disorders
12.03   Schizophrenia Spectrum and Other Psychotic Disorders
12.04   Depressive, Bipolar, and Related Disorders
12.05   Intellectual Disorder
12.06   Anxiety and Obsessive-Compulsive Disorders
12.07   Somatic Symptom and Related Disorders
12.08   Personality and Impulse-Control Disorders
12.10   Autism Spectrum Disorder
12.11   Neurodevelopmental Disorders
12.13   Eating Disorders
12.15   Trauma- and Stressor-Related Disorders

13.00   Cancer (Malignant Neoplastic Diseases)
13.02   Soft Tissue Cancers of the Head and Neck
13.03   Skin
13.04   Soft Tissue Sarcoma
13.05   Lymphoma
13.06   Leukemia
13.07   Multiple Myeloma
13.08   Salivary Glands
13.09   Thyroid Gland
13.10   Breast
13.11   Skeletal System—Sarcoma
13.12   Maxilla, Orbit or Temporal Fossa
13.13   Nervous System
13.14   Lungs
13.15   Pleura or Mediastinum
13.16   Esophagus or Stomach

13.17   Small Intestine
13.18   Large Intestine
13.19   Liver or Gallbladder
13.20   Pancreas
13.21   Kidneys, Adrenal Glands, or Ureters--Carcinoma
13.22   Urinary Bladder--Carcinoma
13.23   Cancers of the Female Genital Tract—Carcinoma or Sarcoma
13.24   Prostate Gland--Carcinoma
13.25   Testicles
13.26   Penis
13.27   Primary Site Unknown
13.28   Cancer Treated by Bone Marrow or Stem Cell Transplant
13.29   Malignant Melanoma

14.00   Immune System Disorders
14.02   Systematic Lupus Erythematosus
14.03   Systemic Vasculitis
14.04   Systemic Sclerosis (Scleroderma)
14.05   Polymyositis and Dermatomyositis
14.06   Undifferentiated and Mixed Connective Tissue Disease
14.07   Immune Deficiency Disorders, Excluding HIV Infection
14.09   Inflammatory Arthritis
14.10   Sjogren's Syndrome
14.11   Human Immunodeficiency Virus (HIV) Infection

Residual Functional Capacity (RFC)

Before moving on to Step 4, there is an intermediate determination that must be made about your Residual Functional Capacity (RFC)— that is, what you can still do mentally and physically on a regular and continuous basis despite your severe medical conditions.[11] The SSA looks at your "exertional" and "non-exertional" limitations to determine what you are still capable of doing. This is an assessment of the most common work activities an individual can perform on a regular and continuous basis, taking into account all evidence of all physical and mental impairments and related symptoms—whether sever or non-severe.[12] Common exertional limitations include difficulty with lifting, carrying, standing, and walking, while non-exertional limitations include almost everything else, from bending, to grasping objects, to mental aptitudes like maintaining concentration.[13]Environmental limitations and sensory limitations can also reduce one's functioning and must be considered.[14]

At this step, the SSA looks at all of the evidence in the file to determine how much you can lift, and then classifies your lifting ability as Sedentary, Light, Medium, Heavy, or Very Heavy, where Sedentary requires lifting no more than 10 pounds at the most, and Very Heavy requires lifting up to 100 pounds. In addition to physical and mental limitations the Social Security Administration considers how other factors impact your ability to function, like pain and side effects from medication. Once they assess your RFC, they move on the Steps 4 and 5 of the sequential evaluation process.

Step 4: Ability to do Past Relevant Work (PRW)

At Step 4 of the evaluation process, Social Security determines whether someone with your residual functional capacity could perform your past relevant work. Past relevant work is work that you have done within the last 15 years that lasted long enough for you to learn how to do it, and in which you earned substantial gainful activity. The SSA will look

---

[11] 20 CFR § 404.1545
[12] 20 CFR § 404.1545(a)(1); SSR 96-8p(5)
[13] SSR 96-8p
[14] 20 CFR §404.1545(d)

at all such work and classify the physical and mental demands associated with these jobs. If someone with your limitations could do any of that work on a full-time basis, you will be denied.

It is important to note that they look at your ability to perform your past work as you performed it and as it is generally performed in the economy. They do not care about your ability to perform your specific job at a specific company or your ability to get hired. Rather, they will look at it in the context of how the job is normally performed in the economy. If they determine that you cannot perform any of those jobs, they move on to the next step. If you can go back to one of your jobs, as you performed it, or as it is customarily performed in the economy, you will be denied.

Step 5: Ability to do Other Work

The last step is where most cases are decided. At Step 5, the SSA looks at your ability to perform other work that exists in significant numbers in the economy. They have a limited burden to show that—considering your age, education, and work experience—you are unable to engage in other work. In order to be found not disabled, you must be able to engage in full-time work as it is normally performed. Therefore, if you can perform only part-time work, you may still be found to be disabled.

Medical Vocational Rules

Individuals who are 50-years old or older have a significant advantage over younger individuals at Step 5, because the SSA applies special medical-vocational rules commonly referred to as Grid Rules.[15] The logic behind these rules gives credence to the notion that the older one is, the less education one has, and the fewer skills one has from past work or training, the less likely it will be for her to engage in other competitive work available in the economy.

At this step, the SSA looks at your RFC, which they determined prior to Step 4, the highest level of school that you completed, and the skill level of your past work. Skill level is classified according to Specific Vocational Preparedness (SVP), which is the time that it takes to obtain

---

[15] 20 CFR Part 404, Subpart P, Appendix

average proficiency in a particular occupation. The more skills that you have acquired in your past work, the more likely it will be that these skills would allow you to perform other work at a lesser physical level than your past work.

Let's look at an example. Mike the janitor is 52 years old. He suffered a severe back injury that limits his ability to stand, lift, bend, stoop, crouch, and crawl. As a result, he is capable of performing no more than Sedentary work, which requires lifting 10 pounds at the most and very little standing. He graduated from high school, and has worked in janitorial services for the last 15 years. This job requires the ability to lift up to 50 pounds, and is therefore a Medium level job. Mike is clearly unable to meet the physical demands of that job, because he is limited to lifting no more than 10 pounds. The janitorial job is listed as a semi-skilled job, but it does not have skills that transfer to any sedentary jobs. Under the medical-vocational rules, Mike should be found disabled and win his case.

In addition to the medical vocational profiles listed, there are two special profiles that also result in disability.[16] If you have a marginal education and a 35-year history of arduous, unskilled, physical labor, but are no longer able to do this type of work, you will be found disabled, even if you could perform some other work. The second special vocational profile that results in disability is an individual who is at least 55 years old, has a limited education, and has no past relevant work experience in the last 15 years.

It can be very difficult for younger individuals (those who are 49 and under) to win at this step, because they must prove that they cannot perform even Sedentary, unskilled work. Sedentary work requires lifting no more than 10 pounds, standing only 2 hours total out of an 8 hour day, and very little postural activities like climbing, balancing, kneeling, crouching, or crawling.[17] These are sit down jobs in which one is lifting very negligible weight like files or small tools. The most common limitations that impact this level of work are difficulties using one's hands, visual limitations, the necessity to elevate one's feet for extended periods of time due to swelling, and cognitive impairments. The complete inability to stoop also significantly impairs one's ability to perform Sedentary work.[18]

---

[16]   20 CFR § 404.1562

[17]   SSR 96-9p.

[18]   SSR 96-9p.

SEDENTARY RFC

RULE	AGE	EDUCATION	PREVIOUS WORK EXPERIENCE	DECISION
201.01	Advanced age (55-59)	Limited or less	Unskilled or none	Disabled
201.02	Advanced age	Limited or less	Skilled or semiskilled– skills not transferable[1]	Disabled
201.04	Advanced age	High school graduate or more - does not provide for direct entry into skilled work[2]	Unskilled or none	Disabled
201.06	Advanced age	High school graduate or more - does not provide for direct entry into skilled work[2]	Skilled or semiskilled– skills not transferable[1]	Disabled
201.09	Closely approaching advanced age (50-54)	Limited or less	Unskilled or none	Disabled
201.10	Closely approaching advanced age	Limited or less	Skilled or semiskilled– skills not transferable	Disabled
201.12	Closely approaching advanced age	High school graduate or more - does not provide for direct entry into skilled work[3]	Unskilled or none	Disabled
201.14	Closely approaching advanced age	High school graduate or more - does not provide for direct entry into skilled work[3]	Skilled or semiskilled– skills not transferable	Disabled
201.17	Younger individual age (45-49)	Illiterate or unable to communicate in English	Unskilled or none	Disabled

LIGHT RFC

RULE	AGE	EDUCATION	PREVIOUS WORK EXPERIENCE	DECISION
202.01	Advanced age (55-59)	Limited or less	Unskilled or none	Disabled
202.02	Advanced age	Limited or less	Skilled or semiskilled– skills not transferable	Disabled
202.04	Advanced age	High school graduate or more - does not provide for direct entry into skilled work[2]	Unskilled or none	Disabled
202.06	Advanced age	High school graduate or more - does not provide for direct entry into skilled work[2]	Skilled or semiskilled– skills not transferable	Disabled
202.08	Advanced age	High school graduate or more - provides for direct entry into skilled work[2]	Skilled or semiskilled– skills not transferable	Disabled
202.09	Closely approaching advanced (50-49)	Illiterate or unable to communicate in English	Unskilled or none	Disabled

MEDIUM RFC

RULE	AGE	EDUCATION	PREVIOUS WORK EXPERIENCE	DECISION
203.01	Closely approaching retirement age	Marginal or none	Unskilled or none	Disabled
203.02	Closely approaching retirement age	Limited or less	None	Disabled
203.10	Advanced age	Limited or less	None	Disabled

ASCEND
DISABILITY LAWYERS LLC

RFC REQUIREMENTS

SEDENTARY	
Sitting	6 of 8 hours
Standing and walking	2 of 8 hours
Lifting and carrying	Under 10 pounds frequently
LIGHT	
Sitting	2 of 8 hours
Standing and walking	6 of 8 hours
Lifting and carrying	10 pounds frequently, 20 pounds occasionally
MEDIUM	
Sitting	2 of 8 hours
Standing and walking	6 of 8 hours
Lifting and carrying	25 pounds frequently, 50 pounds occasionally
HEAVY	
Sitting	2 of 8 hours
Standing and walking	6 of 8 hours
Lifting and carrying	50 pounds frequently, 100 pounds occasionally

AGE DEFINITIONS

Younger	18-49
Closely Approaching Advanced Age	50-54
Advanced Age	55-59
Closely Approaching Retirement Age	60-64

EDUCATION DEFINITIONS

Illiterate	Little or no formal schooling; inability to read or write simple instructions
Marginal	6th grade education or less; ability to do simple, unskilled jobs
Limited	7th-11th grade education; ability to do most semi-skilled and some skilled tasks
High school and above	12th grade education; ability to do semi-skilled and skilled work
Inability to communicate in English	Inability to speak, read, and understand English; difficulty doing a job regardless of education if unable to communicate in English

WORK EXPERIENCE DEFINITIONS

None	No past relevant work
Unskilled	Experience has been in work that requires little or no judgment; simple duties can be learned and performed in a short period of time
Skilled or semiskilled—skills transferable	Work experience involves exercising judgment in determining which machine or manual operation must be performed to achieve certain results, or in dealing with personnel, or abstract ideas at a high level of complexity. More than 30 days are required to achieve average successful job performance. The skills learned can be used in other semiskilled or skilled jobs within claimant's RFC
Skilled or semiskilled-skills not transferable	Work experience as above, but the skills cannot be transferred to other work in RFC

ASCEND
DISABILITY LAWYERS LLC

CHAPTER 3

Substance Abuse & Failure to Follow Prescribed Treatment—Two Things that Can Get You Denied Regardless of the Severity of Your Medical Condition

> *"Numbing the pain for a while will make it worse when you finally feel it."*
> —J.K. Rowling, Harry Potter and the Goblet of Fire

Drug or Alcohol Abuse (DAA)

Drug and alcohol abuse can cause serious problems for disability claimants, particularly those alleging disability due to mental impairments. If SSA decides that you are disabled, but that you suffer from medically documented drug or alcohol addiction, they must then determine whether the addiction is a contributing factor to your being disabled. [19] The key factor in determining whether the substance abuse is a contributing factor to your disability is whether your disability would still exist if the addiction or abuse no longer existed.[20] If your disability would cease if you stopped using the substances, then you will be found not disabled. However, if your condition would continue to be severe, even in the absence of drug or alcohol addiction, you will be found disabled.

The SSA not only looks at the symptoms and limitations directly related to the substance abuse, but also how it diminishes the therapeutic effect of medications, or otherwise limits your response to treatment. For example, if you suffer from debilitating chronic pain, for which you take narcotic pain medication, drinking excessive amounts of alcohol may limit the effectiveness of the medication. In those cases, your alcohol abuse may

---

[19] 20 CFR 404.1523
[20] SSR 13-2p

be a contributing factor to your disability, because the medication would better control your pain level if you were to stop drinking.

In order to engage in this analysis, the SSA must first establish that your drug or alcohol usage meets the medical definition of a substance use disorder. Therefore, they must have objective medical evidence (signs, symptoms, and laboratory findings), from an acceptable medical source that establishes that you suffer from drug or alcohol addiction.[21] They cannot simply assume that your admitted usage constitutes substance abuse or addiction. It must be documented by acceptable medical evidence.

If you suffer from drug or alcohol addiction, it is very important that you seek appropriate treatment, not only for yourself, but also to support your disability claim. The rules state that one suffering from such a condition must seek appropriate treatment for the addiction, and that the individual must make progress in their treatment for overcoming the addiction.[22] This is even true for those who have already obtained benefits, as benefits can be discontinued for failing to take the proper action identified above.

While the rules concerning drug and alcohol addiction are not intended to be used as a sword to deny claims, and are not meant to serve as a source of moral or social judgment, some individuals in the SSA use it to strike down otherwise worthy claims. In my experience, many Administrative Law Judges apply the rules fairly and as they are written in the regulations. However, one occasionally encounters a decision-maker who will use any mention of drug or alcohol abuse to deny the claim. They seem to do so based on personal, subjective belief rather than the law. In these circumstances it is even more important that you have documentation of ongoing treatment for drug or alcohol abuse, even if you believe that it does not impair your ability to work.

Failure to Follow Prescribed Treatment

Failure to follow prescribed treatment may also result in a denial, regardless of how severe your impairment is. In order to receive or continue receiving benefits, an individual must follow treatment

---

[21] SSR 13-2p

[22] 20 CFR 404.1536

prescribed by her medical providers. The treatment must actually be prescribed by a treating physician, and not merely recommended, and it must be expected to restore one's ability to work.[23]

There are, however, a few acceptable reasons for failing to follow prescribed treatment, including, but not limited to the following: (1) the treatment or procedure is against your religion; (2) the same or a similar surgery was previously performed but was unsuccessful; (3) the treatment or procedure is extremely risky; or (4) you cannot reasonably afford the treatment.[24]

The inability to afford treatment is a commonly encountered issue in disability cases, and requires further discussion. Failure to follow prescribed treatment may be excused in cases where an individual is willing, but unable to afford prescribed treatment, and there are no community resources available from which they could obtain the prescribed treatment.[25] This is one of the most common reasons given by claimants for lack of treatment. In order to use this as a justification, you must document all attempts to obtain treatment at local community clinics, hospitals, and treatment facilities. There must be a significant effort made to obtain treatment, and you must provide evidence of your financial inability to obtain it, preferably by supplying letters from the facilities or agencies that you contacted. You are not expected to travel 500 miles for treatment, but an argument can be made that a hospital or clinic within an hour's drive that will take you at little or no cost would be sufficient, and that you would have some obligation to seek treatment there.

The court also recognizes another reason for failing to follow prescribed treatment when an individual suffers from a psychiatric impairment or a combination of psychiatric impairments that cause the refusal or inability to follow prescribed treatment.[26] This rule provides an example of a mentally disabled individual suffering from schizophrenia, who believes that people are attempting to poison him or her, resulting in refusal to take the medication.[27]

---

[23] 20 C.F.R. 404.1530

[24] 20 C.F.R. 404.1530

[25] SSR 82-59

[26] HALLEX ii-5-3-1

[27] HALLEX ii-5-3-1

CHAPTER 4

How the Process Works

"Rivers know this: there is no hurry. We shall get there some day."

—A.A. Milne, Winnie the Pooh

Initial Application

Everything starts with the application. In order to initiate a claim for disability benefits, one must begin by filing an application in person at a local SSA office or online. Once the application is filed, a representative at the local SSA Field Office will be assigned to the claim. They will collect information and then forward it to a state agency called Disability Determination Services (DDS). DDS is a local state agency in the state in which the claimant resides, and is typically part of the state's Department of Human and Family Services or an equivalent title. Due to the nation-wide backlog, some claims are sent to overflow locations in other states. This agency makes the medical determination, and walks through the 5-Step Sequential Evaluation Process described in the previous chapters. Each Claim is assigned to a Disability Examiner (DE), who is tasked with collecting and compiling evidence, scheduling Consultative Exams when necessary, and rendering decisions based on medical opinions provided by the state agency Medical Examiners. This agency either approves or denies the claim.

Reconsideration

If your claim is approved by DDS, it will typically be sent back to the local SSA Field Office for further processing prior to you receiving your benefits. This is done in conjunction with a regional payment center that handles the release of back payments and ongoing payments. If your claim is denied, you have 60 days from the date of the decision to file an appeal. In most states the appeal is called a Request for Reconsideration, or "Recon" for short. A Reconsideration is similar to the initial application determination, in that it is sent back to DDS and assigned to a different Disability Examiner to review the prior decision and to issue a new determination. In some states, called prototype states,[28] the Reconsideration has been eliminated, and an appeal of an initial determination is treated as a request for a hearing before an Administrative Law Judge.

Administrative Law Judge (ALJ) Hearing

Once the appeal has been processed by the local SSA office, it is forwarded to a hearing office that serves the jurisdiction in which the Claimant resides. These offices fall under the authority of the Office of Hearings Operations, which oversees 10 regional offices, half a dozen national hearing centers, and over 160 hearing offices. As of 2018, there were 1,600 administrative law judges and 9,100 support staff working in these facilities.[29]

All of the evidence that was made a part of the claim at the DDS level is exhibited in an electronic file, and the case will ultimately be assigned to a judge and staff to work it up for hearing. You will have the opportunity to submit additional evidence, and to attend a hearing before an Administrative Law Judge, who will decide the case.

If the judge denies your claim, you have the opportunity to file yet another administrative appeal to the Appeals Council. The appeal must be filed within 60 days of the date of the judge's denial letter. If the Appeals Council refuses to review the claim, you may proceed in Federal Civil Court within the jurisdiction in which you reside, or file a new application.

Timeline and Denial Rates

This can be a long process, so it is important to understand the

---

[28] POMS DI 12015.100 Disability Redesign Prototype States: Alabama, Alaska, California (Lost Angeles North and Los Angeles West Branches), Colorado, Louisiana, Michigan, Missouri, New Hampshire, New York, and Pennsylvania

[29] https://www.ssa.gov/appeals/ho_locator.html

time-frame involved and to know whether or not you have a viable case. It typically takes DDS about six months to decide the initial claim. If the Claim is denied and a Request for Reconsideration is filed, it will take them an additional four months on average to render a decision. Appeals to have the case heard before an administrative law judge can take anywhere between 12 and 24 months to be heard, depending on the particular hearing office to which the case is assigned. If the claim is denied by an administrative law judge, and an appeal is filed, it can take the Appeals Council up to a year to decide whether or not the case should be reviewed and sent back to the judge.

Most people are denied at the initial level, as reported in agency statistics which typically show about a 70% denial rate. The denial rate for Reconsiderations is even higher at nearly 80%. Of those denied at these stages, most do not appeal. Of those who do appeal, 55% of them will be denied nationally. The vast majority of all Appeals Council appeals are denied.

It is easy to become discouraged when you see these numbers. However, it is important to note that those who stick with their claim have a better chance of receiving benefits on average, because they ultimately have the opportunity to have the case reviewed by a highly educated, experienced, and usually fair Administrative Law Judge, who is trained to evaluate all of the evidence in the file.

There are some Claimants who believe that filing multiple successive applications will increase their chances of winning. The thought process seems to be that they will wear the SSA down by sheer persistence and a refusal to give up. This logic if faulty. Multiple applications in and of themselves have absolutely no impact on the likelihood that one will be awarded, and can actually have the opposite effect at the hearing level. Sometimes, peoples' medical conditions worsen, they are diagnosed with additional disabling conditions, or they reach a more favorable age category during subsequent applications, and are awarded as a result. This can lead to the illusion that they were awarded simply because they filed multiple times.

TIMELINE AND STATISTICS

STAGE	WHAT HAPPENS	TIMELINE	
File Initial Application	➤ SSA office processes the application, collects additional information, and submits it to DDS.	30 Days	
Decision on Initial Application	➤ DDS orders medical records, submits forms, and may order Consultative Exam ➤ Submits all evidence to Medical Consultant(s) to rate Disability ➤ DE renders determination	180 Days	70% Denial Rate
Request for Reconsideration *(You skip this stage if you live in Alabama, Alaska, some parts of California, Colorado, Louisiana, Michigan, Missouri, New Hampshire, New York, and Pennsylvania)*	➤ Most states have an administrative appeal called a Reconsideration. ➤ This is essentially the same review process as the initial application, but your case is reviewed by different DDS personnel.	120 Days	80% Denial Rate
Hearing with ALJ	➤ The case is sent to a local hearing office where it is ultimately assigned to a judge for a hearing.	540 Days	54% Denial Rate

*Waiting periods are approximations derived from public data provided by the Social Security Administration and other groups. These numbers fluctuate somewhat. This is designed to give you a general idea of how long the process may take. The SSA is not bound by these time periods and work cases as they receive them.

ASCEND
DISABILITY LAWYERS LLC

Appeal Deadlines

There are important deadlines throughout the case, and denials must be appealed timely. Claimants have 60 days to file an appeal at the Initial, Reconsideration, Hearing, and Appeals Council levels. Failure to file timely appeals is one of the primary reasons that individuals have to start over, but there are exceptions to the rule if one has "good cause." A lawyer can ensure that all appeals are filed in a timely manner.

Sometimes it is also possible to reopen a prior claim. You can reopen a prior application within 12 months of the decision date for any reason. SSDI claims can be reopened within 4 years with good cause, and SSI claims can be reopened within 2 years for good cause.

CHAPTER 5

Filing the Initial Application

"A journey of a thousand miles begins with a single step."
—Lao Tzu

Every claim begins with an application. The application must also be accompanied by a Disability Report that asks for specific information about your medical condition, medications, treatment, hospital visits, and other related matters. SSDI applications can be initiated online at www.ssa.gov, in person at a local SSA field office, or over the phone using the SSA's 800 number. SSI applications cannot be completed online, so you will have to use one of the other methods. However, you can initiate an SSI claim by filing a Disability Report online and indicating that you would like to be contacted by SSA to complete an SSI application. This will trigger an individual at your local SSA office to contact you to schedule a time to provide the information over the phone or in the office.

As a practical matter, it is advisable to file everything that you can online, and to avoid calling the national 800 number. The individuals who answer these lines are poorly trained, and typically do not have the experience necessary to answer more than basic questions. They also typically lack access to information that has already been filed with local SSA offices, and will provide false or incorrect information about the status of pending cases and new claims. Recent studies performed by internal and external quality control agencies revealed that over 40% of the information provided by representatives manning the phones at the national 800 number was inaccurate.

If you are unable to file online or do not have access to a computer, the next best option is to go into your local SSA field office, where you will be able to speak with a trained representative. The SSA offers a convenient online tool called the Social Security Office Locator to assist you in finding the office that serves your area. You can access the locator by going to www.ssa.gov/locator, and entering your zip code. Doing so will pull up the contact information for the office assigned to your area. You can call or visit in person to begin the application process.

What You Will Need to File the Application

Before filing an application, it is helpful to gather the necessary information to make sure that you are able to complete the application in a complete and efficient manner. Gathering the following information will ensure that you provide a complete application:

- Information about your medical providers, including names, addresses, dates seen, and treatment provided
- Work history, including company names, addresses, dates employed, and a description of the job duties
- List of all medications and what they are for, the prescribing doctors, and any side effects experienced
- Names and addresses of alternate contacts and witnesses who have observed your disabilities
- Paystubs for any ongoing work, or work that you performed after you say you became disabled

This is a short list of major components of the application, but there is a good deal more information that will be asked of you. The SSA provides a useful checklist at ssa.gov to help you organize your information before beginning the process. It is very important that you file a complete application. One of the main reasons that claims are denied or delayed is a failure to supply all of the necessary information. A good attorney should do this for you.

What Happens After the Application is Filed

After you file your application online, it is sent to a local SSA office. They will gather all of your information and input it into their electronic system. They will also make an initial determination on whether or not you meet non-medical technical requirements for one or more of their programs. If you pass these technical requirements, they will forward your electronic file to Disability Determination Services (DDS). As discussed previously, the case will be assigned to a Disability Examiner, who will collect and organize your information, send additional forms to be completed by you, and work with you and your medical providers to ensure that DDS considers all relevant medical evidence in your claim.

Consultative Exams

After the evidence has been collected, it will be reviewed to determine whether or not it is sufficient to make a determination. If DDS is unable to obtain sufficient information from the evidence provided by your doctors, they may choose to schedule a Consultative Exam with a doctor, who will examine you to evaluate your physical or mental medical condition and comment on your functional capacity. Before scheduling a Consultative Exam, they will consider your existing records, your allegations on any forms submitted as part of the claim, and any other pertinent evidence in the file.[30] If they are unable to resolve inconsistencies in the medical evidence or if the medical evidence is insufficient to make a determination, they will order a Consultative Exam at their expense.

From a practical standpoint, these exams are almost universally bad for your case. Many states only use a handful of doctors. While the doctors are technically independent of the SSA, they become de facto employees of the organization, because the majority of their practice involves conducting these exams. As a result, they have a tremendous pecuniary interest in the process. In my state, there is a clinic that performs nearly 50% of the exams requested in this region, and the reports are rarely favorable for my clients. I have contacted them to determine whether or not the physician is a practicing physician, and have been informed that she has not taken new clients in years. Her practice is set up exclusively to handle Consultative Exams for the SSA.

While the regulations provide that a claimant's own medical source is the preferred source of a Consultative Exam—as long as the source is qualified, equipped, willing to perform the examination or test for the amount SSA is willing to pay, and generally produces complete and timely reports[31]—it has been my experience that they rarely even attempt

---

[30] CFR 404.1519a
[31] CFR 404.1519h

to contact a treating source. I imagine that this is for practical reasons, namely that most practicing physicians working in an institutional setting or in private practice are extremely busy and do not have time to respond to such requests, much less provide the level of reporting required by the regulations. After all, most doctors get into the practice of medicine in order to actually practice medicine and heal people, not be mired in paperwork and litigation.

Once your Consultative Exam report has been submitted to DDS, a Medical Consultant employed by the state agency will review all of the evidence in the file to determine how severe your impairments are and to provide an opinion as to what you are still capable of doing from a physical and mental standpoint, in spite of your functional limitations. This assessment is referred to as your residual functional capacity, or RFC. The DE will then apply the rules and regulations to the evidence in your file, incorporating the opinions of the Consultative Exam doctor and the non-examining state agency medical consultant, to determine whether you are disabled under their rules.

One of the most common reasons that claims are denied at this level is a claimant's failure or refusal to supply necessary information. It is extremely important that you reply promptly to all correspondence from the DE, particularly questionnaires that they ask you to complete, such as the Function Report and Work History Report. Failure to turn these in can and does result in a denial. When you are represented, DDS is supposed to contact your attorney directly, and should not contact you, unless you have given them permission. Unfortunately, this rule is rarely followed.

CHAPTER 6

The Hearing & the Administrative Law Judge

"A judge can't have any preferred outcome in any particular case. The judge's only obligation—and it's a solemn obligation—is to the rule of law."

—Judge Samuel Alito, Supreme Court Justice

The majority of initial applications and reconsiderations are denied, and require an appeal to have the case heard before an Administrative Law Judge. These appeals are processed by an individual hearing office in your area called the Office of Disability Adjudication and Review (ODAR). ODAR must grant your request to have your hearing heard before an ALJ unless a fully favorable decision can be rendered without having a hearing. At the hearing, you will have an opportunity to present additional evidence, testify about your situation, and offer witness testimony.

Most people have never been in court, so they draw their expectations from what they have seen on popular day-time television. Disability hearings are much different. They are non-adversarial in nature, which means that there is not an opposing attorney representing the government. The rules of evidence are relaxed, and evidentiary and procedural objections are rarely lodged. The court rooms are more akin to small conference rooms than actual court rooms, and they are private. You will never have a jury or a member of the general public sitting in on the case. There is usually a marked absence of yelling, flowery or fiery oration, and lengthy cross-examination. These hearings typically last an hour or less. While this is not like Law and Order, it can be a little bit like Judge Judy in the rare case that you have a hostile and unprofessional ALJ presiding, but those judges are rare.

The ALJ is typically a very educated and experienced lawyer, and the vast majority of them conduct hearings in a professional and courteous manner. They are under tremendous pressure to decide an ever-increasing number of cases each year, so they may seem a little absent, cold, or rushed on occasion, but this is the nature of their position. They have a limited amount of time to perform their duties, which primarily include developing the record in a fair and impartial manner and rendering a decision based on their assessment of the record as a whole. They review all of the evidence "de novo," which means "anew." They are not bound by the prior determinations made in your case, including the DDS determination, and have the power to draw their own conclusions from the evidence without being hindered by a prior determination. Judges are held to an incredibly high standard in issuing supportable legal decisions. This is a daunting task when one considers that most ALJs issue 500 or more hearing decisions per year. Some judges render upwards of 700 decisions!

As in life, there are counterexamples to the professional and fair ALJs that one typically encounters. Whether you agree or disagree with their assessment of the case, most ALJs seem to exhibit a fair balance between applying the law, protecting the trust fund, and serving the public. However, there are some outliers in most offices. These ALJs have unusually high denial rates, and some are openly hostile or aggressive towards claimants and their attorneys. There is not much that can be done in these situations, other than going into the hearing knowing that you are essentially preparing the case for appeal. There are even larger societal implications when you encounter an entire ODAR where this behavior and mindset seems to be part of the administrative culture from the top down.

The Vocational Expert

Other than the judge, a court reporter, and your attorney, the Vocational Expert (VE) is the only other person who typically attends and testifies at the hearing. VEs are responsible for classifying your past work and for responding to the judge's hypothetical questions about your ability to perform that work and other work in the economy, given your limitations. VE testimony can make or break your case.

The questioning is done in a very choreographed manner, in which the VE responds only to hypothetical questions, and does not discuss you as an individual. This is because the VE is there to provide vocational information only, and cannot form an opinion as to your particular limitations. The ALJ is the one who decides what kind of functional limitations you have, and then poses various questions to the Vocational Expert, incorporating those limitations. For example, a judge may ask a VE to assume that a hypothetical individual can lift 10 pounds, can sit for 6 out of 8 hours in a day, can stand for 2 hours in a day, can occasionally climb ramps and stairs, but never climb ladders, ropes or scaffolds, can reach overhead occasionally, and can understand and remember simple one to two-step instructions. She will then ask the VE if such a hypothetical individual with those particular limitations could perform your past work or other work in the economy.

Notice that the judge does not refer to you in particular. This is to ensure that the VE does not make an independent assessment of your particular abilities, because this is an issue reserved for ALJ only. A VE can never form an independent opinion about your medical condition or limitations. A good attorney will be prepared to cross-examine the VE when necessary, and to pose his or her own hypothetical questions that incorporate all of your limitations.

Topics Covered at the Hearing

The hearing is designed to be a fact-finding proceeding, in which you will testify about a number of different things relevant to your case. While every judge runs her hearings a little bit differently, most hearings follow a similar pattern of questioning. Among other things, you will be asked about the work that you performed over the last 15 years (Past Relevant Work), the date you stopped working and why, severe impairments and symptoms, types and outcome of treatment, functional limitations, side effects from medications, daily activities, like cooking, cleaning, and preparing meals, hobbies, and difficulty with personal care such as showering or bathing.

CHAPTER 7

The Appeals Council

If the ALJ denies your claim, you can submit an appeal of the decision to the Appeals Council headquartered in Falls Church, Virginia. Your case will be assigned to an appeals judge, who will determine whether or not the ALJ's decision should be reviewed. They will review the decision only on one of the following grounds: (1) the ALJ abused her discretion; (2) the ALJ committed an error of law; (3) the decision is not supported by the substantial evidence in the file; or (4) the decision raises a broad public policy issue.

They have several options. They can deny the request for review, affirm the judge's decision, modify the decision, reverse and remand the case to the judge for further proceedings, or reverse and approve the case. In reality, the Appeals Council rarely grants a request for review, and it can take them 12 months to tell you so. The best that most people can hope for is a remand to the ALJ, which sometimes gives them another bite at the apple. If the Appeals Council denies your request for review, you can pursue the matter further in Federal Court or you can file a new claim, but the Appeals Council level is the final administrative remedy, and the case cannot go further within the SSA's administrative decision-making structure.

CHAPTER 8

Proving Your Case

"The interest I have to believe a thing is no proof that such a thing exists."

—Voltaire

You are responsible for proving your own case. While the SSA and DDS have an obligation to assist you in obtaining necessary evidence, particularly medical evidence, it is a limited burden, and at the end of the day, you are responsible for supplying this information. To win your case, you must show, "by a preponderance of the evidence," that you are disabled under the rules and regulations. This burden is met when "such evidence as a whole shows that the existence of a fact to be proven is more likely than not."

Medical evidence from acceptable medical sources is the most important evidence in your case. Acceptable medical sources include licensed physicians (MD or DO), licensed psychologists, licensed optometrists, licensed podiatrists, licensed advanced practice registered nurses or other advanced practice nursed within their scope of licensure,[32] and licensed physicians assistants within their licensed or scope of practice.[33]

Along this line, medical opinions can be extremely valuable and must be assessed by the decision-maker. The SSA used to give some level of deference to your own treating doctor's opinions, but regulations enacted in March of 2017 have eliminated such deference. In evaluating medical opinions about your functional limitations, decision-makers must consider a number of factors, including supportability, consistency with other medical evidence, and the doctor's relationship to the claimant.[34] They will look at the length of the treating relationship, the

[32] For claims filed after March 27, 2017
[33] For claims filed after March 27,2017
[34] CFR 404.1520c

frequency of examinations, the purpose of the relationship, the extent of treatment and examinations, the examining relationship, and the doctor's specialization. Out of all of these factors, the emphasis is on supportability and consistency.

CHAPTER 9

Credibility—A Term of Art

"Don't pee on my leg and tell me it's raining."
—Judge Judy Sheindlin

One of the most important considerations at your hearing and in the decision-making process is your credibility. While the SSA does not technically call it a credibility assessment anymore, that is essentially the purpose of the hearing. It is to determine whether or not your subjective allegations regarding the nature, severity, and frequency with which you experience severe functional limitations is supported by the evidence and is consistent with the record as a whole. The worst thing that you can do in your case is exaggerate or lie about your symptoms, because all experienced ALJs are good at uncovering dishonesty and exaggeration. If you have a worthy case, this type of behavior will only detract from the veracity of your claims. Tell the truth, always.

Credibility is really a term of art, as it is not defined in the regulations. Decision-makers are given wide latitude in making this assessment, but they must follow certain guidelines. In determining whether your limitations are as bad as you say they are, the SSA engages in a specific decision-making process. They first determine whether or not there is an underlying medically determinable impairment that could reasonably be expected to produce the symptoms.[35] There must be medical sings or laboratory findings from an acceptable medical source to substantiate the diagnosis. For example, if you say that you have severe back pain that makes it difficult for you to stand and sit for prolonged periods of time, you need diagnostic imaging that reveals an underlying condition like degenerative disc disease or a herniated disc.

Once the SSA determines that these symptoms are reasonably expected, given your underlying impairment, they will evaluate the

---

[35] CFR 404.1521

intensity and persistence of those symptoms.[36] They look at the medical evidence, doctors' statements, daily activities, types, dosages, and effectiveness of medications, treatment and response to treatment, and accommodations that you make to deal with your symptoms. In evaluating this evidence, consistency is the most important consideration.

---

[36] CFR 404.1592

CHAPTER 10

How to Speed Things Up

The application and appeals process can take a long time. There is really no getting around that fact. Everyone is in a virtual line, waiting for their cases to be decided. The best way to speed things up is to supply all information to the SSA when requested. Other than that, there are only a few regulatory mechanisms that can be used to expedite a case when particular criteria are met.

Dire Need Requests

Claimants who lack access to food, shelter, or life-sustaining medicine can request that their claims be expedited due to dire need. Mere lack of income or resources does not qualify under this provision, because most claimants going through the process are under tremendous financial strain.

Compassionate Allowances

The Compassionate allowance program is designed to quickly identify very serious conditions or illnesses that would almost universally result in the Claimant meeting or equaling a Listing, and therefore result in disability benefits being awarded, even though all of the objective medical evidence has not yet been received. There are over 200 diagnoses that qualify under this program, including numerous forms of cancer, heart conditions, lung disease, and other more obscure diseases. You do not have to do anything to have your claim identified as a Compassionate Allowance Case. SSA actively screens and flags applications with these diagnoses.

TERI Cases

TERI is short for terminally ill, and is used to expedite cases in which the individual suffers from a diagnosis that is likely to result in imminent death. The following diagnoses, conditions, and medical situations qualify as TERI cases:[37]

- An allegation from the claimant or third party that the illness is terminal
- An allegation or diagnosis of amyotrophic lateral sclerosis (ALS), known as Lou Gehrig's Disease
- An allegation or diagnosis of acquired immune deficiency syndrome or acquired immunodeficiency syndrome (AIDS)
- Receiving inpatient hospice care or is receiving home hospice care—e.g., in-home end of life counseling or palliative nursing care
- Chronic dependence on a cardiopulmonary life-sustaining device
- Awaiting a heart, heart and lung, lung, liver, or bone marrow transplant (excludes kidney and corneal transplants)
- Chronic pulmonary or heart failure requiring continuous home oxygen and an inability to care for personal needs
- Any malignant neoplasm (cancer) which is: Metastatic (has spread); Defined as Stage IV; Persistent or recurrent following initial therapy; or inoperable or unresectable;
- Cancer of the esophagus
- Cancer of the liver
- Cancer of the pancreas
- Cancer of the gallbladder
- Mesothelioma
- Small Cell or Oat Cell lung cancer
- Cancer of the brain
- Acute myelogenous leukemia (AML) or acute lymphocytic leukemia (ALL);
- Comatose for thirty (30) days or more
- Newborn with a lethal or congenital defect.

---

[37] POMS: DI 23020.045 (TERI)

Wounded Warriors

Veterans who sustained injuries while on active duty after October of 2001 may be eligible for expedited processing of their applications.

100% Permanent and Total Veterans Disability Rating

SSA expedites applications from veterans who have received 100% Permanent and Total disability ratings from the VA.

CHAPTER 11

How a Lawyer Can Help

"I shall pass this way but once; any good, therefore, that I can do or any kindness that I can show to any human being, let me do it now. Let me not defer nor neglect it, for I shall not pass this way again."

—Etienne De Grellet

Not all lawyers and law firms are created equally. In addition to legal expertise and skill, it takes a tremendous amount of effort, organization, and innovation to handle cases. Just because a lawyer is great in the court room, does not mean that your case will be a winner. The hearing is the tip of the iceberg. Most successful legal matters take months of preparation, coordination, follow-up, customer service, documentation, collecting evidence, and research. It takes a team to win, and the relationship can last for months or years, so evaluate the entire firm carefully. The lawyer you see on T.V. with an aggressive nickname, wearing the fancy suit, yelling like a madman, will probably never even look at your case. It is the associate attorneys and staff who will do that. The way that they have been hired, trained, and compensated matters more than anything. Treat the relationship like a partnership or marriage. It takes two. See the next page for a list of qualities to look for in a firm.

10 THINGS TO LOOK FOR IN A LAWYER

1 **Industry Specific Relevant Experience** What percentage of his or her practice is devoted to Social Security Disability?

2 **Litigation Experience** Most Social Security Claims end up going to court. How many SSD hearings has the attorney been to?

3 **Good Support Team** It's not just the lawyer who will handle your case. It takes a team to make sure that everything is handled correctly. Who else will you be working with? Will there be a specific point person or Case Manager who responds to your inquiries and questions?

4 **Personal Representation at Your Hearing** Will the lawyer you hire be in court with you, or will it be someone you have never met or spoken with before? How familiar will that individual be with you case?

5 **Great Online Reputation & Service** Look at their Google Reviews. Check their Facebook profile. See what past clients are saying. Do they generally receive 4 and 5 stars and do people actually write reviews?

6 **Excellent Legal Writing** Make sure that any lawyer you hire guarantees that he or she will submit a well-written brief to the judge that discusses your medical records in detail. It is surprising how many fail to do this. Your case demands it.

7 **Communication** They return phone calls within 24 hours and respond to your questions directly.

8 **Transparent and Simple Fee Agreement** Their Fee Agreement or Contract is straightforward, and in plain English, and they are willing to share it with you without question.

9 **Straight Shooters** Are they honest with you about the merits of your case? Do they share the good, the bad, and the ugly?

10 **Caring and Understanding** How they treat you says a lot about the quality of representation that you will get. Make sure that you evaluate this during all initial conversations with the firm. How the receptionist treats you is a good indication of how your lawyer will treat you. It starts at the top.

ASCEND
DISABILITY LAWYERS LLC

Clients Rights and Responsibilities at Ascend Disability

At Ascend Disability, we have gone to great lengths to build a quality team, and to ensure that everyone's primary focus is on winning the case and doing our best to leave our clients in a better position than when we found them. We make sure that all of our people understand our mission. We have codified this as a set of promises or guarantees to our clients, but we also expect our clients to live up to their responsibilities. If you decide to hire an attorney to help you with your claim, make sure that you know what to expect before you sign a retainer.

Client's Rights

1. You have the right to our loyalty. We are your attorneys and serve your legal interests above all else.
2. You have the right to confidentiality. You can disclose information pertinent to your case knowing that it will remain confidential. We protect your personal and health information as if it were our own.
3. You have the right to accessibility. Your phone calls are returned promptly, and you may speak with your attorney when needed. While other staff are critical to the development of your case, your attorney is in charge and is happy to speak with you.
4. You have the right to an experienced attorney and knowledgeable, competent staff.
5. You have the right to our respect. You will never be talked down to or judged. We are in this business to build up, not tear down. Gossip or negativity about a client will get someone fired in our office, regardless of how good they are at their job. That is our line in the sand.

6. You have the right to direct communication and honesty. We will always be honest with you about the merits of your case. We will never lead you on. We will only agree to represent you if we think that your case can be successful and it will put you in a better position.

7. You have the right to decide. We are on your team. While we will always offer our best advice, you have the ultimate right to decide.

8. You have the right to a fair fee agreement written in plain English. There are no hidden fees or unexpected costs.

9. You have the right to compassion and empathy. Everyone needs help sometimes. Every single one of us. There is no shame in asking for it when you truly need it.

Client's Responsibilities

1. You have the responsibility to be respectful to our staff. Respect always goes both ways.

2. You have the responsibility to communicate directly with your attorney and to be honest in all dealings. We cannot help you if we do not know the truth.

3. You have the responsibility to let us know if you are not satisfied in some way. We cannot fix what we do not know.

4. You have the responsibility to respond to requests for information, so that we can effectively develop your case.

5. You have the responsibility to notify us of significant changes in your situation.

6. You have the responsibility to keep fighting. The law is hard, but life is harder. We will never give up on you, but you cannot give up either.

7. You have the responsibility to only seek help when it is truly needed. We cannot help everyone, so we must chose to help those who truly deserve it.

10 WAYS A LAWYER CAN HELP YOU WIN YOUR CLAIM

1 Your odds of winning increase.
An experienced attorney and a well-trained team can increase your odds of winning at both the application level and the appeal level.

2 We handle the entire application for you.
A good lawyer will ensure that all of the information in your application is correct and complete and will submit it to the Social Security Administration electronically to ensure that it is promptly reviewed.

3 We pick the best possible date that you say you became disabled.
There are many rules, regulations, and laws dealing with when you allege you became disabled. If the date you list on your application is either too soon or too late, your application may be denied.

4 We make sure nothing falls through the cracks.
It is surprising how many people are denied, because the Social Security Administration does not get all of the information needed to fully evaluate the case. We perform continuous follow ups throughout the case to make sure that they receive all of the pertinent information necessary to make a decision in your case.

5 If you are denied, we file an electronic appeal immediately.
Many people give up after their claim is denied, because they do not realize that their chances of winning are much better if they stick with it when represented. Many others miss important deadlines, and have to start over.

ASCEND
DISABILITY LAWYERS LLC

6 We develop all of the necessary medical evidence at the hearing level.

Good cases are built on solid evidence. We not only handle this for you, but we also send specific forms to your doctors based on your particular medical conditions.

7 An experienced attorney fights for you at your hearing.

We prepare you for your hearing, and then fight for you once there. The attorney not only ensures that your testimony is beneficial, but also cross-examines the government's experts.

8 A lawyer's services are free if you don't win.

Lawyers who handle this type of work do so on a contingency basis at a percentage established by the Social Security Administration. This provides a strong incentive for attorneys to offer the best representation possible. Think of this as insurance.

9 A lawyer costs the same whether you hire one at the beginning of the claim or wait until your application is denied.

Over 70% of all people are denied on their initial application. Most lawyers refuse to handle initial applications, because they are very time consuming and the odds of success are low. Good lawyers handle the entire claim from start to finish, and establish a solid foundation for appeal if you are denied.

10 An attorney makes sure that you receive the benefits that you are owed.

If you win your case, your attorney reviews the court's decision to assure that the government calculates your monthly payments correctly, and to make sure that you receive all of the back payments that you are owed.

ASCEND
DISABILITY LAWYERS LLC

ABOUT THE AUTHOR

Jason Harmon is the founder of Ascend Disability Lawyers, LLC, which has offices along the Gulf Coast. Originally focusing exclusively on Social Security Disability, Jason has expanded his practice to include Veterans' Disability Benefits, Long Term Disability, ERISA claims, and other employer related issues that the working man or woman commonly face when he or she is no longer able to work.

Jason was born and raised in New Orleans, Louisiana. He attended college at Texas Christian University in Fort Worth, where he double-majored in English and Psychology. After college, he worked for a law firm as a non-attorney representative, traveling to over 300 disability hearings around the country, and writing briefs for the law firm. The firm went on to become one of the preeminent SSD firms in the country.

Soon thereafter, he attended Mississippi College School of Law, where he held leadership positions in numerous organizations, including the Moot Court Board. During Law school, Jason continued to represent disabled individuals in their hearings, and also served as a Guardian Ad Leitum in the law school adoption clinic, assisting the court with placing children in good homes. He graduated from Law School with honors.

After graduation, Jason founded Ascend Disability Lawyers in New Orleans. The firm has expanded to include satellite offices along the Gulf Coast. His firm has helped thousands of individuals fight for their

Social Security disability benefits, and he has personally represented clients in hundreds of hearings. When he is not working in his business or on his business, Jason enjoys spending time with his family, cooking, shooting, fishing, and writing.

About the Coauthors

Tiffany Tate Logan

Tiffany Logan serves as an Attorney Representative and Intake Specialist at Ascend Disability Lawyers, LLC. She has served in numerous capacities at Ascend Disability, including medical evidence review, brief writing, and hearing representation for disabled clients. Prior to this role, Tiffany founded Tate | Logan, P.L.L.C, a Texas-based law firm focusing on matters related to criminal law, probate and personal injury.

Tiffany attended Baylor University, where she majored in Psychology and Minored in Criminal Justice. She went to law school at Loyola University College of Law in New Orleans, where she served in a number of leadership roles, including Association of Women Law Students student bar association representative, president of the Black Law Student Association, secretary of the Association of Women Law Students, secretary of the International Law Society, and moot court staff member. In her final year, she served as South Regional Black Law Student Association Thurgood Marshall Mock Trial Competition Director, Inns of Court member, as the brief writer on the winning team at the 2010 Tulane Law School Moot Court Mardi Gras Invitational Sports Law Competition, and as clinical practitioner in both criminal defense and tax.

At present, Tiffany serves as a 2018 New Leaders Council Fellow, Screener for the New Orleans Film Society, and Praise Team Member for two music ministries: Irish Channel Christian Fellowship and Rhema Ministries.

Clara Van Horn

Clara currently serves as Senior Case Manager at Ascend Disability. As a licensed attorney, she is responsible for overseeing the processing of Social Security Disability claims from the Initial Application through the Hearing Level. Clara's experience and compassion are absolutely critical in this role.

Prior to joining Ascend Disability, Clara worked for a boutique plaintiff's firm in Oxford, Mississippi. She attended Millsaps College in Jackson, Mississippi for both her undergraduate and her graduate degrees. In 2011, she earned her BBA with a major in Business Administration and a minor in Spanish Language and Literature, and in 2012, she graduated with her Masters of Business Administration. In 2013, Clara attended law school at the University of Mississippi School of Law, and graduated with her Juris Doctorate in May of 2016.